The Elephant

A ZEBRA BOOK

Written by Margaret Lane
Illustrated by David Wright

PUBLISHED BY

WALKER BOOKS
LONDON

Millions of years ago there were elephants on every continent of the world except Australia and Antarctica. Some of them, called Woolly Mammoths, have been found frozen whole in northern ice, while the bones of early elephants have been discovered in Europe and North and South America.

Today only two kinds of elephant survive – the African, which is the larger of the two, and the Asian (or Indian) elephant, which has the more docile nature.

African elephant

The Indian elephant has lived and worked with man for thousands of years, and still does. Both kinds are sociable creatures and highly intelligent. They have remarkable memories.

Indian elephant

The elephants' true home is tropical forest and grassy plain, where they live on leaves, twigs, grass and tree-bark, wild fruit and roots. But since man has taken over so much of the earth for his own use, the elephant now must live mainly in nature reserves and grow used to tourists.

Apart from their huge size, the most remarkable thing about elephants is their trunk. This has gradually evolved from the nostrils and upper lip and is as sensitive as a nose, as powerful as a hand and arm.

The trunk gathers and places food in the elephant's mouth, sucks up water for drinking and pours it down his throat.

An adult female is the most important member of an elephant group. She leads and protects the herd – her own young calves of different ages, her grown-up daughters and their young, and other females.

The chief bull elephant, once he has mated with the leading cow, moves off nearby on his own or with other young males under his authority.

The normal lifespan of an elephant is the same as ours – 60 to 70 years. Young elephants can mate and give birth by the age of 16, but are not fully grown until 25 years old. A calf is born about 20 months after mating. The baby stands about one metre tall, has a hairy coat and weighs as much as a full-grown man.

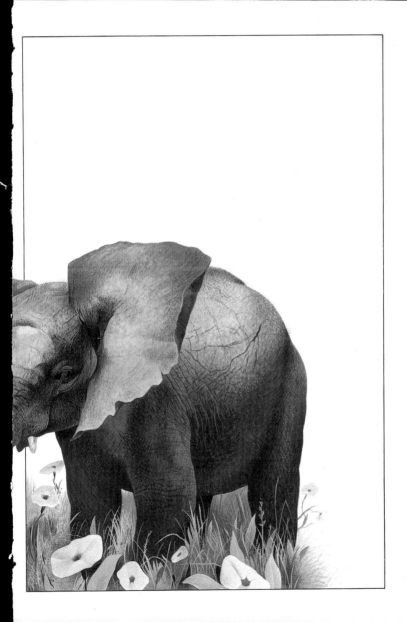

The mother elephant takes great care of her baby. Accompanied by one of her daughters or an 'auntie' elephant, she walks with him between her legs for protection, feeds him with her own milk (he suckles with his mouth, not his trunk) and with an occasional slap teaches him how to behave.

Within the family group, elephants show a great fondness for one another. If a mother elephant dies or is killed, another female immediately adopts her calf. The leading one can be very fierce, flapping her great ears and trumpeting if there is a threat from a human hunter or a lion.

The elephant's weapons are the tusks and the heavy feet. The ivory tusks are a kind of teeth, which grow longer and longer with age.

The powerful feet can trample an attacker into the ground, but are so softly cushioned that a whole herd can troop through the forest without making a sound.

Elephants need so much food that they spend most of the day browsing and chewing, and sleep very little. Their greatest pleasure is bathing, wallowing in pools and rivers and showering water over themselves with their trunks, then spraying sand and dust on their wet skins.

They are good swimmers, but also walk across river beds with only the tip of the trunk held above water.

A herd can travel many miles in a day, sometimes pushing over trees with their heads to reach the high leaves and fruit, and raiding farmers' crops.

Because of their strength and intelligence, elephants have been captured and tamed by man for thousands of years. In ancient times they were used in warfarc, and still play their part in eastern processions, painted and adorned with jewels and silk, as moving thrones for princes and maharajas.

In some circuses, even today, elephants are kept in unnatural conditions to perform unnatural tricks, but this custom is dying out.

They are cruelly slaughtered by poachers for their ivory, but in countries where they live and work with man they have become his friend.